American Bobwhites and Other Quail

by Dr. R.W. Shufeldt

with an introduction by Jackson Chambers

This work contains material that was originally published in 1914.

This publication is within the Public Domain.

This edition is reprinted for educational purposes
and in accordance with all applicable Federal Laws.

Introduction Copyright 2016 by Jackson Chambers

Self Reliance Books

Get more historic titles on animal and stock breeding, gardening and old fashioned skills by visiting us at:

http://selfreliancebooks.blogspot.com/

Introduction

I am pleased to present yet another title on Raising Quail.

This volume is entitled "Quailology" and was published by Fred Kerr in 1903.

The work is in the Public Domain and is re-printed here in accordance with Federal Laws.

As with all reprinted books of this age that are intended to perfectly reproduce the original edition, considerable pains and effort had to be undertaken to correct fading and sometimes outright damage to existing proofs of this title. At times, this task is quite monumental, requiring an almost total "rebuilding" of some pages from digital proofs of multiple copies. Despite this, imperfections still sometimes exist in the final proof and may detract from the visual appearance of the text.

I hope you enjoy reading this book as much as I enjoyed making it available to readers again.

Jackson Chambers

American Bob Whites and Quails

By Dr. R. W. SHUFELDT, C.M.Z.S.
Fellow Amer. Ornith. Union, Hon. Member Royal Australasian Ornith. Union, Etc.

WITH ILLUSTRATIONS FROM DRAWINGS AND PHOTOGRAPHS BY THE AUTHOR

Part I—INTRODUCTION

IN former articles of mine, published in the Outer's Book, I have described and figured all of our United States species of ducks and grouse, with the various allies of the latter group. Similar papers have also been prepared and illustrated on the American species of geese, and these will appear in this magazine later on this year.

It is my intention, in the present series of articles, to describe, figure, and give data, for the purpose of identification, of all of our species of bob-whites and quails. Fortunately I can illustrate these articles throughout with reproductions of photographs made by myself direct from the living birds, and for the opportunity to do this I am indebted to Mr. Edward S. Schmid, the veteran bird fancier of Washington, D. C. There are but two exceptions to this statement, one being the picture presented of Mearns' quail, which is reproduced from a photograph I made of this species of a specimen belonging to the United States National Museum—a favor for which I must thank the late Dr. G. Brown Goode. The second exception is seen in the beautiful picture, illustrating the present Part, of a male bob-white, taken in the act of incubating. This is reproduced from a photograph from life, made some time during the middle of August, 1901, by Mr. George E. Moulthrope, of Bristol, Connecticut, where this interesting case occurred.

Our bob-whites are not true quails, the latter birds being well exemplified in the quail of Europe,—a species I shall touch upon, and present figures of from life, further on in the present series of articles. Nor are our bob-whites *true* partridges, as the latter belong to the genus *Perdix*, an excellent example of which is seen in the common gray partridge of Europe (*Perdix cinerea*).

"Colin" is also a name applied to our bob-whites, and sometimes even made to include the western quails, as the "mountain" and "valley" species. English ornithologists are especially given to the use of this term with respect to our bob-whites, while we very rarely hear it used in this country. Further on we shall see that all of our bob-whites are contained in the genus *Colinus*—hence 'colin.' The origin of this word is interesting, for we find it to be derived from the old French *Colin*, and hence the surname *Collins* in English (*Colas* is the diminutive of Nicolas).

Bob-whites are known as "partridges" throughout the Southern States; they are called "quails" in the Middle Atlantic States and in New England, or in such districts where the ruffed grouse is called a partridge, —the latter being known as a pheasant in the south. This is all well enough so long as the fact is understood that we have no true partridges in the United States; that the habitats of the true quails are in the Old World; that the birds we call pheasants in the East are *grouse*, and that the pheasants (*Phasianidæ*) are Asiatic forms, though the family includes the pea-fowls, the wild and domestic fowls or chickens, the peacock and their various allies.

All of our game birds of these groups are arrayed in the Supersuborder (XV) GALLIFORMES and belong in the suborder (XXIV) *Gallinæ;* in this suborder we have the family (V) *Odontophoridæ*, created to contain all of our bob-whites and quails. This classification takes into consideration the structure or morphology of these birds rather than a grouping of them according to the first chapter of Genesis.

Birds of this family represent and have been arrayed in *five* well-marked and distinct genera; these have been named *Colinus, Oreortyx, Callipepla, Lophortyx,* and *Crytonyx,* and I shall take them up in this sequence in the remaining parts of the present series of a slight projection of rock just above the water, and took careful aim at it with one of my lower extremities. I made a good shot, so that while I felt, and can feel today all of the symptoms of that bath, I did not get it. While I was mentally drying off, I clambered laboriously to the top of the boulder to see if anybody was looking, and my conscience was eased very considerably by finding that I had been unobserved. The rock suffered no ill effects whatever from my slide.

John was not quite so fortunate. He attempted to walk a spruce pole which had been placed across one of the falls, and fell in part way. These experiences, however, only increased our already tremendous appetites, so that when we arrived at the dinner table which was set and surrounded by all of the grandeur that a wild and uninhabited country can give, we made away with enough food for six ordinary men. Our good guide Tuffy had to fry more of the speckled beauties or go hungry. Often times I marvel at the appetite of a man who has the hunger of the tired fisherman, and wish that I could carry back with me to civilization the keen delight with which I attack almost any food in such a place.

After dinner we did not do much fishing. We did not come to kill more than we could use, but only to enjoy ourselves. We smoked our pipes, told a few stories, and later in the afternoon started back toward the boat. I remember that as we left the mouth of the river we gave chase to a fish-duck and her brood of young. It is marvelous with what speed these little ducks can go through the water, and row as we might, we could not catch them. I remember in regard to those stories, that Mr. Booth said the trout bit so rapidly and so savagely at the lower pool that he could scarcely bait his hook fast enough to satisfy the fish; and at one time, in order to keep from being severely bitten himself, he said he had to turn his back to the pool while baiting his hook; but, of course, Mr. Booth has some reputation as a story teller.

Mr. Booth reached the yacht before we did, and had his creel deposited on the back deck. As we stood in silent wonder looking into that famous creel, I could not help but feel in the fullest sense of the word, that Mr. Booth's nick-name was well taken. I felt as though the Booth Fishery Company was actually present.

After dinner that evening the band played. It was the band's final appearance. The band-master felt that it was to the best physical interests of the band that they should make no more appearances, as the captain had had strict orders to allow no more unnecessary noise on the boat.

(TO BE CONTINUED)

Fig. 1.—TEXAS BOB-WHITE. MALE

articles. In doing so I will briefly describe each species and subspecies, giving its life-history, the origin of its name, its range, and how each may be distinguished from any of its relatives, or, in other words, the key to its identification.

Bob-whites and quails are not difficult to distinguish from the grouse or other birds belonging to the *Tetraonidæ*, for the first not only possess naked feet, but the *nasal fossæ* are likewise devoid of feathers. The Texas bob-white, here shown in Figure 1, exhibits this nakedness of the feet (including the tarsi) and nostrils very well. When we come, however, to draw hard and fast lines between our bob-white and quails and the pheasant-group (*Phasianidæ*), it is by no means such an easy matter. Without going into the scientific particulars involving this point— for it would avail us nothing here—I may say that there are not a few birds in various parts of the world, as in India, Ceylon, Africa, China, Formosa, and other countries, which present characters (both internal and external) that render it a very puzzling matter for the ornithologist to accurately determine to which family—that is the *Odontophoridæ* or the *Phasianidæ*—they belong. However, I have already shown how to distinguish the former from our grouse (*Tetraonidæ*), and there can certainly be no danger, in so far as the readers of this article are concerned, of mistaking any of our bob-whites or quails for a guinea-fowl, much less for a wild turkey or peacock, all of which latter are phasianine birds and not perdicine species.

It is needless to say that there is an enormous literature extant on game birds as a whole, and for a goodly share of this our bob-whites and quails come in. They have been written and talked about ever since the first discovery of America, but it has only been within comparatively recent time that we have come to know these birds intimately.

Any intelligent sportsman is more or less familiar with the *habits* of this assemblage of birds that are found where he habitually hunts. There is, however, one interesting habit that is exemplified on the part of the male bob-white, and maybe on the part of other species; I refer to the fact that the male will, sometimes, for one reason or another take upon himself the duty of incubation. An example of this is well shown in Figure 2 of this Part. Should hatching take place while the eggs are being covered by the male, it would be interesting to know how he would behave. I believe that he would lead off the chicks just like the hen bird, and remain near the nest until her return, which, under ordinary circumstances—and she were

able and living—would not be for any great length of time.

Among the game birds of the world there are not a few instances where the male of the species assists in incubation. In the case of our bob-whites, Wilson, the ornithologist, did not appear to know, in so far as we can judge from his published writings, that the male quail assisted in the matter of incubation. Audubon knew about it, and says in his "great work" that "The female prepares a nest composed of grasses, arranged in a circular form, leaving an entrance not unlike that of a common oven. It is placed at the foot of a tuft of rank grass (see Fig. 2) or some closed stalks of corn, and is partly sunk in the ground. The eggs are from ten to eighteen, rather sharp at the smaller end, and of a pure white. The male at times assists in hatching them." This very indifferent description will probably stand pretty well for one case in several hundred, and it would appear that Audubon met with but few nests of this species in his rambles. He reserved most of the space that he devoted to the life-history of this famous little game bird, to describe the capture of it by driving bevies of them into nets. This practice seemed to amuse him very much indeed, as it might the average market-man today, were "quails" plenty enough for them to resort to it.

This is what Audubon says on this point when endeavoring to describe the note of the bob-white: "A fancied similarity to the words 'bob-white' renders this call familiar to the sportsman and farmer; but these notes are always preceded by another, easily heard at a distance of thirty or forty yards. The three together resemble the words 'Ah, Bob White.' The first note is a kind of asperation, and the last is very loud and clear. This whistle is seldom heard after the breeding season, during which an imitation of the peculiar note of the female will make the male fly toward the sportsman who may then easily shoot it."

This is interesting, apart from any other consideration; for it gives us in his own words the fact that he, Audubon, was not above shooting quails during the *breeding season*. But in a way he informs sportsmen (?) that it can be done and *how* it can be done. In this connection I may say that, in a previous article in Outer's, I pointed out that Audubon for the *sake of amusement*, used to go out *at night* with some negroes and catch *dozens* of prairie chickens or pinnated grouse in a fish seine, apparently only for such "sport" as he found in the practice, and he was only deterred in such an outrageous procedure by the merriment of the *negroes* (!), or as he

Fig. 2.—MALE BOB-WHITE (C. V. virginianus) INCUBATING

puts it—after thus capturing more birds than ten families could use—"but now we gave up the sport on account of the loud bursts of laughter from the negroes, who could no longer refrain." (Vol. V., p. 98). American sportsmen need not be surprised at this narrative; for it was Audubon who was so fond of shooting scores of the beautiful white egret (the plume-hunters' victim) during the breeding season, when they had both eggs and young, so he could gratify the demands of the ladies of Charleston for "many of their primary feathers for the purpose of making fans." (Vol. VI., p 135).

Quails of the genus *Callipepla* are very different looking birds as compared with any of the bob-whites,—a fact that can very readily be appreciated by comparing Figures 1 and 3 of the present Part. Indeed, these scaled quails, as they are called, look more like some little species of grouse than they do like a bob-white. Notice in my photograph the beautiful crest the bird has, and the fine emarginations of the feathers of the underparts, causing them to resemble scales and suggesting the name for the members of this genus. These scaled quails are birds that habitually live in the desert regions of the West, and later on I will give the life histories of the two subspecies found in certain localities of the southwestern part of the country, where they are well known to the sportsmen of those parts where they occur.

"Valley quails" are of the genus *Lophortyx*, and they stand among the most beautiful of the smaller game birds of the Pacific region, where they are still to be found in many localities. Unfortunately, they are now rapidly being exterminated, and, unless they are fully protected for a series of years, they will entirely disappear. Think of one of the most elegant game birds in the world actually being wiped off the earth entirely through man's agency; and when once gone, it can never be restored again. Further on I shall present reproductions of photographs of some superb specimens of this genus from life, together with a full account of the members of the genus. This also applies to the mountain and plumed quails of the genus *Oreortyx*, of which, as we know, there are some beautiful varieties or subspecies in western Oregon and the Californias.

Lastly, I shall give a brief history of those gorgeous little quails of the genus *Cyrtonyx*, found in certain parts of Texas, New Mexico and adjacent regions. In my own opinion, these stand among the most beautiful of our quails, yet this fact is not often mentioned, and apparently for the sole reason

Fig. 3.—SCALED QUAIL OF WESTERN TEXAS. MALE

that they are so *tame* and afford the sportsman but little sport in their hunting.

Most, if not all, of these various kinds of quails are easily raised in confinement; if properly cared for and placed under suitable conditions, they may be raised in large numbers. This is now being done with our eastern bob-whites in many places, and the results are most gratifying. Such a culture should be taken up and encouraged with respect to the several western forms, and that before they are all exterminated.

American Bob-White and Quails

By DR. R. W. SHUFELDT, C. M. Z. S.

PART II.—THE BOB-WHITES

WITH ILLUSTRATIONS FROM PHOTOGRAPHS BY THE AUTHOR.

IN Part 1 of the present series I have already presented some interesting facts in regard to our Bob-whites, while in the present Part it is my intention to give a more or less complete history of these birds.

We have, in the first place, *two* species of Bob-whites in the United States avifauna, the first being *the* Bob-white, and the second the Masked Bob-white. Scientifically the Bob-white is everywhere known as *Colinus virginianus* (of Virginia), its specific name having been bestowed upon it by Linnæus, who, however, placed the group in the genus *Tetrao*, under which name the old-time ornithologists arrayed all birds that were at all grouse-like.

This Bob-white ranges all over Eastern North America, from southern Maine, westward through South Dakota, and southward to include Florida. It is also found in the Gulf States to include all suitable localities through Texas, and, beyond our borders, in eastern Mexico. In this very extensive range, the birds, in divers areas, have come to assume fixed, and at the same time different plumage characters. This has given rise to three very distinct subspecies of *Colinus virginianus*—that is, distinct when selected from their "range centers;" for the birds, in any particular case, shade almost imperceptibly into the subspecies of the next contiguous range. Then there are four or five species found in Mexico and Yucatan, all being quite distinct; but with these we have nothing to do here. Further on I will discuss our subspecific forms and their ranges; but let us first turn our attention to the characters as a whole as found in the genus.

We will note in *Colinus*, then, that the feathers of the crown are somewhat lengthened, and, while erectile, do not form a true crest. In the matter of general plumage, it is much variegated, being of a reddish chestnut brown with black and white markings. There are twelve tail-feathers, and, when stretched out, the feet reach beyond them. They lay, in a nest on the ground, from twelve to eighteen white, pyriform eggs, and the downy little chicks are very pretty and extremely active when first hatched.

Colinus virginianus virginianus is *the* type subspecies of the genus, and its range is now rapidly extending westward, to such an extent, indeed, that Coues, in the fifth edition of his "Key," says that its range is "Eastern United States, North to Maine, Ontario, and Minnesota. West to high central plains in South Dakota, Kansas, Nebraska, Indian Territory, Oklahoma, and eastern Texas, and all the while steadily extending in that direction with the settlements and railroads; it has already got beyond the limits assigned in the Key in 1884, and has been introduced and become acclimated in various parts of Colorado, New Mexico, Utah, Idaho, California, Oregon and Washington. I shot it at Fort Randall, S. D., in 1872-73." Both in its normal habitat and wherever introduced it becomes resident, breeding throughout the range.

In the adult male the forehead, line over each eye, and throat are pure white with a bordering of black; crown, neck and breast, reddish-brown; under-parts light tan or tawny-whittish, all the feathers being marked with black in the form of double crescentic bars; under tail coverts, reddish; broad, reddish-brown stripes on sides; dorsum variegated with black, stone gray, deep chestnut and buffy, which last forms a bar on either wing.

This coloration of the plumage is much subdued in the female; the black markings are less pronounced, and, what is to be noticed almost at once by any observer is, that the throat is of a buffy shade instead of white as in the male.

A male Bob-white has a length of about ten inches to ten and a half, the female being about half an inch shorter.

It is not an uncommon thing to find abnormally plumaged birds of this species among the hundreds of scores shot in this country every year. We must meet with albinoes; some melanotic ones, and others exhibiting other phases of abnormal plumage. Sportsmen should preserve such specimens, and,

while they have no scientific status whatever, they are, nevertheless, of value and most assuredly interesting.

In the lower two-thirds of the peninsula of Florida we meet with the first subspecies of Bob-white, which is the Florida Bob-white (*C. v. floridanus*). This variety is not found anywhere else in this country, though it approaches the Cuban quail in appearance (*C. cubanensis*). It is a smaller and much darker bird than the one just described, the male being about the size of the female of *C. v. virginianus;* moreover, in it the bill is jet black and heavier, and the black markings more conspicuous by being broader. Its habits are about the same.

When on the ground our Bob-whites have a very different appearance from some of the western quails, for example such as any of the scaled quails. This will at once be appreciated by comparing the birds figured in figs. 4 and 5.

As I have before remarked, these scaled partridges or quails always remind me of some small form of grouse, and to this the specimen here shown in fig. 5 forms no exception.

Our last subspecies of Bob-white is the Texas subspecies (*C. v. texanus*) of which it is said that it ranges through southeastern New Mexico to southern Texas, and from these regions southward through certain parts of old Mexico. This Texas Bob-white is a species about the size of the Florida subspecies (Fig. 4), and, instead of being a darker form than the Common Bob-white, it is a much paler one. Indeed, the prevailing shade is *gray* rather than a brown, and there is a considerable shading of tan or tawny in the plumage of its upper parts. This subspecies I have had in confinement for several days at a time, during which period I made a number of negatives of it. The one shown in Fig. 4, selected from the lot, makes the bird appear to be much darker than it really is, so much so that it would stand pretty well for a specimen of the Florida Bob-white. This bird, however, was taken in central Texas along with many others, and shipped to Mr. Schmid by one of his regular collectors.

It has the same habits as our quail of the

FIG. 5. CHESTNUT-BELLIED SEALED QUAIL (*CALLIPEPLA SQUAMATA CASTASTANOGAS-TRIS*). MALE. SHOWS THE APPEARANCE OF THE BIRD ON THE GROUND.

eastern States, and its nest and eggs differ in no respect whatever from those of that bird. In fact, as we come northward and eastward, it gradually shades into the stock species—that is, into *Colinus v. virginianus;* and, as we go south into Mexico, it is said to gradually approach *Colinus graysoni* in form and plumage.

In November, 1913, when walking through the woods and fields with my wife near Somerset, District of Columbia, and without any dog, I put up three fine bevies of quails, or partridges as they are known in that locality. There were some thirty in the first bevy, and from a dozen to fifteen in the other two, making fully sixty birds altogether.

The largest flock of these birds I ever saw was flushed by a train of cars on the Union Pacific Railroad, and I saw them from one of the car windows. It was sometime during the latter part of the seventies, and I was traveling westward through Nebraska. The train had stopped "to water" at one of the big tanks close to the rails. No building or people were within miles and the birds had collected in the shadow of the tank, from off the surrounding prairies to enjoy the cool shade, and to drink the water which had dripped from the tank. As the train approached, the entire flock took wing together, and it was truly a most remarkable sight, for there must have been at least over a thousand birds in the bunch!

Wilson's account of the Bob-white is a most interesting one, and especially so for the reason that the species was so plentiful during the time he wrote. He records several instances where the clutch of eggs of a quail was hatched out by the common hen; and, what was still more remarkable, where quails would sit on hen's eggs, hatch them out, and rear the brood of chickens. In one case of this kind, the quail led the brood into the woods, and the chickens soon acquired the habits of young quails.

In commenting upon this, Wilson says: "A friend of mine, who himself made the experiment, informs me, that, of several hen's eggs which he substituted in place of those of the Partridge, she brought out the whole; and that, for several weeks, he occasionally surprised her in various parts of the plantation with a brood of chickens; on which occasions she exhibited all that distrustful alarm, and practiced her usual manœuvres for their preservation. Even after they were considerably grown, and larger than the Partridge herself, she continued to lead them about; but, though their notes or calls were those of common chickens, their manners had all the shyness, timidity, and alarm of young Partridges; running with great rapidity, and squatting in the grass exactly in the manner of the Partridge. Soon after this they disappeared, having probably been destroyed by dogs, by the gun, or by birds of prey. Whether the domestic fowl might not by this method be very soon brought back to its original savage

FIG. 6. MASKED BOB-WHITE (*COLINUS RIDGWAYI*). MALE, FEMALE AND YOUNG MALE. BY THE AUTHOR AFTER ALLEN'S COLORED PLATE.

state, and thereby supply another additional subject for the amusement of the sportsman, will scarcely admit of a doubt."

This is somewhat of a hard story for me to believe, and I am rather inclined to think that Wilson's "friend" was putting one up on him.

Neither Audubon nor Wilson knew of the Quail next to be noticed, which is the remaining species to be described in our list of United States Bob-whites. This is the beautiful masked Bob-white, named by Brewster *Colinus ridgwayi* in honor of Professor Robert Ridgway, our most distinguished living describer of the birds of this country. There is a good account of this bird in Allen's paper on the species (Bull. Amer. Mus. Nat. Hist., July, 1886, pl. 23); it was the colored Plate in this paper which I selected to copy to obtain my illustration for the present Part (see Fig. 6).

This elegant quail formerly ranged from the middle part of the southern border of Arizona, southward to the central region of southern Sonora. From all accounts, however, I fear that it has been entirely exterminated within the boundaries of the United States, which is a great pity, for it is even a handsomer bird than our famous Bob-white of the middle and eastern sections of the country. This masked Bob-white is closely related to Grayson's Quail *(C. graysoni)* of Mexico, and when first introduced into our Check Lists, was mistaken for it, a mistake which has since been corrected.

In addition to the name I have given for it, it is likewise known as Ridgway's Colin, Arizona Bob-white, and the Hooded Quail. Coues says that the female of this species so closely resembles that sex of *C. v. texanus* "as not to be readily distinguished." In it the irides are brown, the bill black, and the feet horn-color. Further, it is easily distinguished from all others of our Bob-whites by the black of the front and sides of the head and neck, and, in some individuals, by the narrow white line over the eye (Fig. 6). Beneath, the parts are of a chestnut or cinnamon color, which is unspotted and varies in shade, reminding one of the breast of our common eastern Robin. White spots, however, occur on the flanks, these spots generally being on the tips of the feathers, and each bordered anteriorly by a bar of black. The top and back of the head, to include the nape, is light brown mixed with black and white, the last being tinged with yellow. The back of the neck and between the shoulders, reddish-brown shaded with gray; upper parts principally black, variegated with light brown and soiled white. The tail is slate gray on its upper side, where it is dotted with whitish and wavy lines of the same shade; beneath, the markings are somewhat the same but fainter. Wing-coverts, reddish, the feathers being barred with black and bordered with whitish. Primaries, dusky and emarginated internally with whitish.

This much of a description would indicate a Bob-white, in so far as the male bird is concerned, that could in no way be mistaken for any other species than the Arizona Masked one. Should any one hunting in the southern part of Arizona meet with such a bird, it should certainly be reported, and if shot, it should, with still greater certainty, be preserved and scientifically labeled.

FIG. 7. PLUMED QUAIL. (*O. P. PLUMIFERA*). MALE. FROM LIFE BY THE AUTHOR AND REDUCED

American Bob-White and Quails

By DR. R. W. SHUFELDT, C. M. Z. S.

PART III.—MOUNTAIN QUAILS AND OTHER SPECIES

WITH ILLUSTRATIONS FROM PHOTOGRAPHS BY THE AUTHOR.

HAVING completed my account of the Bob-whites in Parts I and II of the present series of articles, I have next to introduce a genus of birds, the members of which stand among the handsomest of the smaller game fowls anywhere in the world. These are the Mountain or Plumed Quails of the Pacific region of the United States, the several forms representing them being included in the genus *Oreortyx*, of which there is but one species (*O. picta*) including the three known subspecies. All of these will be described in the present Part, and in Fig. 7 we have a picture from life of one of them, which gives an excellent idea of the representatives of this group (*O. picta plumifera*).

Oreortyx means a mountain quail, but it is a badly constructed word, as it not only leaves the gender in doubt, but *oros*, a mountain, is

from the Greek, while *ortyx* is the Latin for a quail—the first being masculine and the latter feminine. However, the quails do not seem to mind it, being more concerned about the vicious guns and traps that are now rapidly wiping their beautiful race completely off the map.

The type subspecies of this genus is *the* Mountain Quail (*O. p. picta*), the subspecific name meaning painted or pictured (Latin). It is said to occur, in suitable localities, throughout the "Humid Transition Zone strip of the Pacific coast from southwestern Washington south to Monterey County, California." It also occurs on Vancouver Island as an introduced species.

We have next the subspecies known as the Plumed Quail (*O. p. plumifera*) (from the Latin *pluma*, a plume, and *fero*, to bear), so called on account of its elegant head plume. Further on I shall give the description of these birds, but I desire first to name them and to give the localities where they occur.

This subspecies, in so far as its *range* is concerned, was referred to by Coues, in the last edition of his "Key," as being "the prevailing form on both sides of the Cascade range in Oregon, the Sierra Nevadas in California, and even the Coast Range in the latter State from about latitude 34 degrees to Lower California; in fine, it is the ordinary Mountain Quail of most parts of California, aside from the restricted Coast Range of the preceding, and also the one which extends E. into Nevada. The distinction is a subtle one, but I am willing to let the subspecies pass muster with a hundred others of which I have no favorable private opinion" (p. 758). This subspecies is a good one, Coues' dictum to the contrary, it having been recognized by Gould as early as the year 1837, *not* 1857 as Doctor Coues gives it to us.

Finally, we have the San Pedro Quail, a subspecies confined to "San Bernardino and San Gabriel Mountains, Southern California, south to Hansen Laguna and San Pedro Matir Mountains, Lower California." This bird bears the scientific names of *O. p. confinis,* bestowed upon it on account of its being found on a range which borders or adjoins the range of another subspecies of the same genus (Latin). It was first described by Mr. Anthony in the Proceedings of the California Academy of Sciences (2d series II, Oct. 11, 1889, page 74).

Wilson knew nothing of any of these western quails, as that part of the United States was unexplored in his time; while Audubon's figures of the "Californian Partridge" and the "Plumed Partridge" present so many inaccuracies that it would hardly be a profitable undertaking to occupy valuable space here for their pointing out. His descriptions of these birds are made up from what Townsend wrote him about them, and from a specimen or two he had had loaned him. Audubon also figures a "Welcome Partridge" from "the north-west coast of America" (*Ortix neoxenus*), which was originally described and named by Vigors (Garden and Menagerie of Zoöl. Soc. ii, p. 311), and which may or may not be a young bird of one of the Mountain Quails; in any event, we have no "Welcome Partridge" in this country.

Sometimes they used to put jokes up on Audubon; and many years ago, the veteran taxidermist of New York City, Mr. John G. Bell, who was out West with him on some expedition or other to the Missouri River, once told me how he "fooled old man Audubon with the skin of a vireo" which he, Bell, had so manipulated that it appeared to be a new species!

By referring to Fig. 7 of this Part we may study such of the characters of the form and plumage of one of these Mountain Quails, as will serve as an aid to distinguish any bird of the genus from any other species of the family. It will be noted that the head is not only slightly crested, but it bears likewise a long, backward-extending feather-plume composed of *two* slender, dark-colored or black keeled feathers. They are about three or four inches in length, being longer in the male than in the female, and *normally* appear as only *one* feather, not as two, as drawn by Audubon and followed by Coues without criticism. These birds have stout bills and feet and twelve feathers in the tail. Males and females are alike, barring some slight differences as the one just pointed out. They are big, stout quails of great beauty of plumage, the color areas being definitely massed.

In the Mountain Quail (*O. p. picta*) the throat is of a chestnut color, bordered with black and white, the latter being outermost and continued round under the lower mandible. Forehead, ashy gray; back, wings and tail, olive-brown; upper and lower breast, slatey-gray, shaded above with olive-brown, and marbled below with black in fine pencilings. Tail, fuscous and similarly marked; wings, olive-brown, with the inner secondaries and tertiaries bordered with buff; primary feathers also fuscous, like the body-color of the tail-feathers. Belly, chestnut, with the sides barred with broad bars of black and white (Fig. 7), the latter sometimes shaded with rufous-white, which latter is the color of the feathers of the tibiæ, the flanks, and the hinder abdominal area. Crissum black, lined with clear chestnut, the black having a velvety appearance. Bill dusky, and the feet are of a pale brown. With this description, aided by Fig. 7, any one will be able to pick out a Mountain Quail of the genus *Oreortyx*.

Passing to the Plumed Quail (*O. p. plumifera*), we find that it is very much like the last one described; the olive-brown area, however, is less, and the slaty-gray is correspondingly extended on the back and underparts; forehead, soiled white instead of ashy-gray. In typical cases the back of the neck is like the breast, and not olive-brown like the dorsum in the Mountain variety. I am inclined to think, from what I have read and heard about this subspecies, that, at the limits of its range, specimens are very much like the birds on the contiguous areas; in other words, in some places these various subspecies of *Oreortyx* shade into each other.

It is said that the subspecies named above, the San Pedro Quail (*O. p. confinis*), can only be distinguished by possessing "grayer upper parts and thicker bill," a fact I have never had the opportunity to personally verify. However, the subspecies has been generally recognized by our best ornithologists, and it is therefore quite likely that, in the case of *typical specimens* from the San Pedro Martir Mountains, we will find birds *constantly* exhibiting the characters claimed for this subspecies.

FIG. 8. CHESTNUT-BELLIED SCALED QUAIL (*CALLIPEPLA S. CASTANOGASTRIS*). FROM LIFE BY THE AUTHOR

These birds lay buff-colored eggs, and otherwise present habits of the Quails in general with special ones pertaining to the genus. Much has been published about them, especially in Pacific Coast literature, and to this the reader is referred for further accounts of their life histories. No one with the ordinary powers of an observer could possibly mistake any of the "Mountain Quails" for any one of the "Valley" species, as for instance the California Quail of the genus *Lophortyx*, an example of which I here present in Fig. 9 of this Part, a most gentle little bird which I photographed a number of times while it was in my possession.

Our next genus contains the "Scaled Quails," and the name *Callipepla* (Wagler) has been bestowed upon it, which is a term from the Greek and means beautifully arrayed (*Kallipeplas*).

These birds have long tails composed of *fourteen* feathers—an unusual number for quails. The sexes are very much alike, and both have the emarginated feathers of the lower parts, giving that scaled or shelled appearance which suggested the specific name for the genus (Latin *squamata*, like a scale). They are forms which occur on the southern boundaries of the United States, the range of the Scaled Quail (*C. s. squamata*) having been given as "Upper and Lower Sonoran Zones from central Arizona to western Texas,

north to southern Colorado, and over the most part of the Panhandle of Texas, east nearly to central Texas, and south to the valley of Mexico;" while the Chestnut-bellied Scaled Quail occurs in the "Lower Sonoran Zone of southern Texas, from Eagle Pass and San Antonio south to northern parts of Coahuila, Nuevo Leon, and Tamaulipas."

These Scaled Quails are desert forms, and the sexes are more or less alike—the female being somewhat smaller with a trifle duller plumage. They average about ten or eleven inches in length, and have an alar extent of over fourteen inches.

The Scaled Quail is of a general slaty-blue color, including the soft crest of the head, which latter terminates in pure white (Fig. 8). On the back and wings the gray shades into an olive-brown, becoming redder, posteriorly, beneath the wings. Abdomen buffy and pale-colored. Feathers of neck and lower parts black emarginated, producing the aforesaid scaled appearance. Like the dorsum, the elongated flank feathers are of an olive-brown, with long oval white spots marking each feather, these, in some cases, resembling stripes with edgings of brown. Posteriorly, on the flanks and under tail-coverts the feather-emarginations gradually disappear or become very faintly marked, arrow or heart-shaped markings taking their place. When the wings are closed, either one presents the

FIG. 9. CALIFORNIA QUAIL (*L. C. CALIFORNICA*). MALE.
Note that the feathers of the ornament of the head are drawn together so as to appear as one feather.

lengthwise stripe seen in all of our United States Quail, it being formed by the light-colored edgings of the inner secondary feathers. Tail, lead-colored. Primaries, fuscous and unmarked. These birds lay from eight to sixteen eggs to the clutch in a nest they build on the ground; they are generally of a pale, buff shade and evenly speckled.

Lastly, in this genus we have the Chestnut-bellied Scaled Quail or Partridge (*C. s. castanogastris*), which is a subspecies resembling the former; but the plumage is generally darker, the crown and the dorsum being of the same shade as is the breast and sides of the head. Throat lighter. In the male bird there is an abdominal median area of a dark chestnut color which is conspicuously defined. This is rarely found in any of the females of this interesting subspecies of *Callipepla*.

C. squamata is widely known in the Southwest as the "Blue Quail," and it associates, as I have been told, with Gambel's Quail—that is, *Lophortyx gambeli* of the genus to be described in the remaining Part (IV) of this series of articles.

A good many years ago, when I was serving as Post Surgeon at Fort Wingate, New Mexico, these birds, that is *C. s. squamata*, were not uncommon in the county about forty miles east of the Post on the plains, near a place called Grant; while in the nearby hills the "Fool hen" or Mearns' Quail (*Cyrtonyx m. mearnsi*) was occasionally to be found, that locality being the northern limit of its range in those times.

There is no question but what any of these quails might be successfully raised in captivity, proper regard being paid to their necessities and food. Just at this time there seems to be some evidences that the matter of rearing all kinds of game birds in this way, on public and private preserves, is attracting more general attention, and enterprises of the kind should be encouraged in every possible way.

Fig. 10. California Quail (Lophortyx Californica). Male in Full Plumage. Slightly Less than Half Natural Size. Photo from Life by the Author.

American Bob-White and Quails

By DR. R. W. SHUFELDT, C. M. Z. S.

PART IV.—QUAILS OF THE GENERA *Lophortyx* and *Cyrtonyx*, WITH NOTES ON THE QUAIL OF EUROPE

WITH ILLUSTRATIONS FROM PHOTOGRAPHS BY THE AUTHOR.

IN SO far as authoritative works upon the science of ornithology are concerned, perhaps the most indifferent and downright inaccurate collection of quail pictures extant are the ones to be found in the fifth edition of the "Key to North American Birds" by Elliott Coues. It was surely a great pity to mar such a useful work as that has proved to be by the employment of figures of that character. His own drawings of "Mr. and Mrs. Bob White" are truly ridiculous caricatures of what they were intended to represent. Fig. 508—the Bob-white family—carries idealism to the limit (p. 755); the Masked Bob-white is not recognizable, and the head of Gambel's quail, drawn by the author, is quite incorrect. Moreover, he has drawn the feathers of the plume all standing apart, while under Brehm's wretched figure, on the very next page (Fig. 512), of the "California Helmet Quail," he criticizes this point, remarking that in life "the feathers of the crest are always bundled in a bunch, not standing apart, as in this figure" (p. 759). On p. 760, the figure designated as "Gambel's Quail" is not that bird at all, but a reproduction of a very poorly mounted specimen of the California quail, the white loral stripes being plainly seen. He reproduces in Fig. 511 the incorrect figure of Audubon of the Plumed Quail. In life the feathers of the plume in that species never stand far apart as there represented, while it is quite incorrect in other particulars. Finally, the head of the "Massena Quail" on page 762 is as absurd a

picture as any one would care to see. It has been given a crest of which no quail in the world ever had the like.

These various criticisms are made here for the sole purpose of setting forth the several errors they take into account, in that sportsmen, naturalists and others may not be led astray by them. Through personal examination any competent ornithologist may satisfy himself of their justness.

Coues designated the Valley Quails as "Helmet Quails" for the reason that their "elegant crests" are recurved "helmet-wise." No one else appears to have noticed the resemblance, and so the term has never come into use, in so far as I am aware.

These California or Valley Quail belong to the genus *Lophortyx*, the name being derived from two Greek words meaning a crested quail. The bird shown in Fig. 10 is an excellent example of them, and a well known one of the aforesaid genus. Two species make up the latter, that is, *L. californica* and *L. gambeli*.

Lophortyx californica ranges over the Pacific coast region from Oregon to southern Lower California. It is represented by two sub-species, *L. c. californica*, the type California Quail, it being found throughout the 'Humid Transition and Upper Sonoran zones of the Pacific coast region, from southwestern Oregon south to Monterey County, California; introduced into Vancouver Island, Washington, and Colorado. While the second

sub-species or the Valley Quail (*L. c. vallicola*) occurs in the 'Subarid Upper and Lower Sonoran zones, from the Klamath Lake region, Oregon, south throughout California (except humid coast strip and eastern desert region) to Cape San Lucas, Lower California, and east to mountains of western Nevada.'

Gambel's Quail is a distinct species and a very well known one to sportsmen in California. It was named for William Gambel, the naturalist, as long ago as 1843. It is said to range throughout the 'Lower Sonoran desert region of southern California, southern Nevada, Arizona, and southwestern Utah, east of the southwestern corner of Colorado, and also in southwestern New Mexico to the Rio Grande Valley and the El Paso region of extreme western Texas, and south into northeastern corner of Lower California and to Guaymas, Sonora.'

As elsewhere stated, this bird often associates in flocks with the Scaled Quails on the borders of deserts, and so forth, and in California many know the species as the Top-knot Quail.

Any birds of the genus *Lophortyx* may be known by the form of their crests, as shown in Fig. 10 of this Part. This crest may develop to become an inch in length, being composed of six or seven glossy black, imbricated feathers, there generally being fewer in the crest of the female. As a matter of fact, she is smaller than the male and her plumage is quite different. The tail has from ten to

FIG. 12. COMMON QUAIL OF EUROPE (COTURNIX COTURNIX). MALE. HALF NAT-
URAL SIZE. PHOTO FROM LIFE BY THE AUTHOR.

fourteen feathers—the normal number being twelve—and less or more constitute exceptions. It is about four-fifths the length of a wing, and when the feet are stretched out alongside of it, the toes do not reach to its end.

The male has a deep, jet-black throat and chin, with a white border (Fig. 10). A straight white line from the base of the crest, on either side, backward to the body line. These markings are absent in the hen.

These few characters will place any one of these quails *in the genus*, as compared with any of the others found in this country not belonging to *Lophortyx*.

Coming next to the subspecies, we find that the male of the California Quail has a minute white stripe running from the eye to the bill (Fig. 10). The top of the head is of a sooty-brown, while the forehead is inclined to be whitish, with minute linear markings of black. Neck feathers speckled with white and with dark edging and shaft-lines. Back, ashy-gray, glossed with brownish-olive, the combination resulting in a beautiful shade and is very conspicuous. Breast, slate-color or a slate-blue. Lower breast, deep tan, becoming an elegant golden brown on the abdomen, where the feathers come to have glossy black edges to them. Flank and sides like the dorsum, all the feathers being marked by clean-cut longitudinal stripes of white. Crissum and lower abdominal area, tan-brown with the longitudinal median stripes of the feathers dark, blackish brown.

The rich brown color on the abdomen is wanting in the female, and her breast is of an olive-gray.

Length, ten to eleven inches. Young and chicks have special plumages that need not be described here.

Sometimes, it is said, this species may build its nest in some shrub or even in a tree; but it usually builds on the ground, as in the case of Gambel's and other quails. Eggs, from ten to twenty, pale buff or creamy in color, blotched and spotted all over with spots of various shades of brown and drab. These are beautifully figured in color in Bendire's work, and the variations they present are truly remarkable. Four specimens, natural size, are shown on the Plate, together with the eggs of all of our other quails—a most interesting display.

The Valley Quail (*L. c. vallicola*) is the island bird, and when typical specimens are secured, they are found to be subspecifically perfectly distinct from the last, being lighter in color, grayer on the dorsum and flanks, with some few other color differences, such as the line along the internal edge of either wing being a very pale tan instead of a brownish-olive.

Coues remarks that no specimens, up to his time, were taken that exhibited the slightest intergradation between this form and the one described above. I may say here that, personally, I have never seen one in my lifetime.

As stated before, Gambel's Quail is a very distinct species, and the male may at once be recognized by the little white stripe bethe beak and eye being absent. Moreover, the forehead is black with fine white linear markings. There is no white speckling on the neck, while the top of the head is of a chestnut brown. Above, clear ash, which is also the color of the upper breast. A large, glossy black area on the abdomen, which is lacking in the female. Remaining lower parts whitish, tinged with buff, becoming purplish chestnut on the sides, the feathers being striped with white as in the California Quail. Posteriorly, on the crissum, flanks, and hinder abdominal area the feathers are whitish, and the streaks pale ash or even dusky. Irides, brown; bill, deep black.

In the female the crest is composed of fewer feathers; they are of a dark brown color and do not curl forward as in the male bird. Where the black abdominal area is absent, it is replaced by feathers of a dingy white shade, showing medio-longitudinal dark streaks, the whole constituting a character by which the female of this species may at once be recognized.

The plumages of the young and the chicks are well known, but they need not be described here, and the same applies to the eggs, which are much like those of the California Quail, only their tone is somewhat heavier.

We now come to the genus *Cyrtonyx*, the last of our United States Quails to be described in these articles.

The type subspecies of this genus is an extralimital one, being found only in Mexico (*C. montezumae montezumae*); while our subspecies or Mearns' Quail (*C. m. mearnsi*) occurs from central Arizona and central New Mexico, eastward to central Texas and southward into northern Mexico. This is a big-billed and very remarkable bird with large and extraordinary-looking claws, which last accounts for its generic name (Greek, *Kurtos*, bent; and *onux*, a claw).

As will be observed from Fig. 11 of the present Part, it has a full crest on the occiput composed of soft feathers. There are but twelve feathers in the unusually short tail, it being in life almost entirely concealed by the coverts. Wing-coverts are conspicuously large and quite cover the primaries of the wings.

The characters of the feet are well shown in my figure, as are also the ocellated body-feathers and the remarkable striping of the head in the male bird. Plumage of the female quite unlike that of the male, and she lays pure white eggs without any markings whatever. One of these latter I figured in *The Nidologist* a good many years ago, and Major Bendire also has it in his work.

Mearns' Quail was named by Nelson, the Arctic explorer, in honor of Dr. Edgar A. Mearns of the Army, one of the naturalists who accompanied Colonel Roosevelt upon his African Expedition.

This bird has the prevailing colors of the back much variegated, they being of a rufous, tan, and some black, the shaft-lines of the feathers being buffy or white. Round black spots and black bars on the wings (Fig. 11), these, on each feather, being regularly paired. Below, the dark feathers are each characterized by having paired, *white*, round spots, giving the entire area a white, spotted appearance, which is very striking, not to say handsome. Median line of breast and abdomen, vandyke-brown, while the flanks, sides and area about the vent are shiny black. Occiput, black anteriorly, slightly speckled with white. Crest, brown. Throat, black, and the head striped as shown in Figure 11 with black and white.

Adult female quite unlike the male indicated in the merging of the markings, and the more general fulvous shade to the feathers. Head shows no peculiar markings, and the throat is either light buff or even whitish. Lower parts lighter, and the feathers generally mottled with white and black.

A male bird measures about nine inches in extreme length, and has an extent of about seventeen. No one could possibly mistake one of these quails for any other species, and they are generally known on the ranges in New Mexico and Arizona as "fool quail" on account of the reluctance with which they take wing, and what happens to be a stupid fearlessness of man.

This quail is generally found in wooded districts, ranging up in the mountains for over nine thousand feet. It is by no means gregarious as is the case with other quails, and often only a bird or two will be put up. I have handled it in the flesh only a few times; but I think that, of all the beautiful quails I have ever seen, the male of this species, in full spring plumage, is the handsomest game bird we have in this country.

It makes a neat nest on the ground, and I have already referred to the eggs in a former paragraph.

In closing this account of our United States quails I desire to add a few notes on the Common Quail of Europe.

Coues gives a description of this species in the last edition of his "Key" (Vol. II, p. 751), illustrating it with a figure from Brehm, which is rather indifferent. These birds I have had alive several times, and my photographs of them are reproduced in figures 12 and 13 of the present Part. My chief object in introducing them here has been to show how little they look like any of our American quails. On this point Coues remarks, after stating that the bird occurs in "Europe, Asia, and Africa," that it has been "recently imported and turned loose in considerable numbers in the U. S., as in New England; but its perma-

FIG. 13. COMMON QUAIL OF EUROPE (C. COTURNIX). FEMALE. RATHER MORE THAN HALF NATURAL SIZE. PHOTO FROM LIFE BY THE AUTHOR.

nent naturalization is open to question. If one will compare this bird with Bob White he will see how very different is the Old World Quail from our Colins, or any other birds of this country called 'quail'; but that it resembles these more nearly than the European Partridge, *Perdix cinerea*, does; so that, if we must borrow a name from any Old World birds for our species of *Colinus*, *Lophortyx*, *Callipepla*, etc., the term 'quail' is rather more appropriate than 'partridge.'"

The sexes differ somewhat, while in both the prevailing colors are whitish, buff, black and various shades of brown.

Whether there are any of these quails at large in the country at the present time I am unable to state; it would, however, be interesting to know of this fact.